HAIRY 'N' WEIRD

(the strangest mammals you ever saw)

written by Lisa McCourt
illustrated by Cheryl Nathan

ROXBURY PARK

LOWELL HOUSE JUVENILE
LOS ANGELES
NTC/Contemporary Publishing Group

to the amazing Max Martin Bernstein and his awesome grown-ups
—L.M.

to Tucker Combs—the sweetest little guy—with love
—C.N.

Published by Lowell House
A division of NTC/Contemporary Publishing Group, Inc.
4255 West Touhy Avenue, Lincolnwood (Chicago), Illinois 60712-1975 U.S.A.

Lowell House books can be purchased at special discounts when ordered in bulk
for premiums and special sales. Contact Department CS at the following address:
NTC/Contemporary Publishing Group
4255 West Touhy Avenue
Lincolnwood, IL 60712-1975
1-800-323-4900

ISBN: 0-7373-0404-9
Library of Congress Control Number: 00-132031

Roxbury Park is a division of NTC/Contemporary Publishing Group, Inc.

Managing Director and Publisher: Jack Artenstein
Editor in Chief, Roxbury Park Books: Michael Artenstein
Director of Publishing Services: Rena Copperman

Printed and bound in the United States of America

00 01 02 TWP 10 9 8 7 6 5 4 3 2 1

Who's the fastest, the furriest, the heaviest, the smartest?

Set your Weirdometer to H-A-I-R-Y because it's time for more outrageous fact-finding! Each of the creatures you'll meet in these pages is hairy and weird. But some are weirder than others. Which ones will rate the highest on YOUR Weirdometer?

Use a sheet of paper to give each warm-blooded beast a number from one to five according to your gut feeling. Then ask a friend to do the same.

Since we all have different ideas about what's weird to us, your friend's answers will probably be different from yours. What's gross and freaky to one person could be lovably strange to another!

VAMPIRE BAT

Eeek! This little weird one is scary stuff! A vampire bat's favorite food is—you guessed it—BLOOD!

This one-ounce mini-monster hangs upside down all day in caves or hollow trees. Its hooked claws lock into place so that it can sleep without worrying about falling off its perch. Then, as darkness falls, the vampire bat swoops down in search of a tasty, bloody meal.

But the bat can't even see its victim! Instead, it lets out a high, squeaky call, then listens for the echoes that come back. Based on these echoes and its awesome sense of smell, the bat zeroes in on its prey—usually a cow, pig, or horse. The bat's teeth are so sharp that the victim barely feels the bite. After making a wound, the bat laps up the blood—sometimes filling its belly so much that it almost can't fly afterward!

CHIMP

Chimps are known to hug, kiss, cuddle, and hold hands! They communicate with special sounds that mean danger, sorrow, or excitement. They even use body language the same way we do. A hand outstretched means "food, please!"

Chimps who have been raised by humans have learned to become amazingly human-like. One of the most awesome things they have been taught to do is speak sign language! A chimp named Washoe learned over 300 signs and even made up her own signs for things she didn't know how to say. For example, she called a fizzing soda a "listen drink," and a duck on a pond a "water bird." Washoe and two other signing chimps taught a baby chimp 58 words in sign language (even though the baby had never seen humans sign the words).

When they are given paints and other art tools, chimps can even create art! Some consider the work of certain chimps to be very good, and there have been all-chimp exhibits in some famous art galleries.

In the wild, chimps live in communities of up to 80 members, but they usually move around in smaller groups within the community. Sometimes two chimps become best friends, doing everything together. A mom will always stay with her babies until they are around seven or eight years old.

KOALA

Koalas are often called bears, but they're not members of the bear family. They're actually marsupials—a fancy word for mammals that carry their babies in a pouch. Kangaroos are the most famous marsupials, but other animals, such as Tasmanian devils, opossums, and nearly all the mammals living in Australia, are also marsupials.

When a koala baby is born, it is smaller than a gumball! It crawls out of the mom's body, up along her belly, like a little bug until it finds her pouch. The baby then crawls in and latches onto a teat—a place on the mother's body where the baby can suck milk. Once the baby starts sucking, the mom's teat swells inside the baby's mouth and safely holds it in place that way for the next seven to eight months.

By the time the baby is ready to peek out of the pouch, it is a furry, fully-formed little animal. But even after that first peek, it might not leave the pouch for a while. And once it does come out, it'll still hop back in when it wants to rest or drink milk, for another month or so. To hitch a ride, the baby hugs its mom's belly for a while, but soon learns to crawl up on her back. Then mom and baby travel through the trees together with baby on piggyback until the baby is ready to be on its own.

Koalas are lazy. They spend almost their whole lives just sitting around in trees. They have a special inch-thick pad of fur that cushions their bottoms so they always have a cozy seat to sit on!

GIANT ANTEATER

Would you believe this silly-looking thing could scare away a hungry jaguar? The giant anteater can grow longer than six and a half feet from head to tail. When it rises up on its hind legs and lashes out with its powerful claws, it can make a predator think twice.

Since those long, sharp claws are so important, the anteater protects them by walking on its knuckles and on the sides of its hands. (That's a pretty weird-looking walk.)

So you'd think such an intimidating creature would be an awesome hunter, right? Well, guess what he hunts? Yep, ants. First, he sniffs out some yummy ants with his super-sensitive nose. Next he uses those handy claws to rip the nest open. Then it's time to whip out the anteater's weirdest weapon—his tongue, which is over two feet long! The tongue reaches deep into the ants' nest and catches the little treats with the tiny spines and sticky spit that cover it. Then the anteater sucks the tongue back up into its mouth and swallows the ants. It takes a lot of ants to fill up an animal this big. But that's no problem. The anteater can flick its tongue in and out of the nest 150 times every minute!

FENNEC FOX

This little fox only stands about eight inches tall at its shoulders, but its humongous ears can be six inches long or more! Aside from making it look irresistibly cute, the ears serve two important functions.

The first is to keep the fox cool in the hot desert regions where it lives. Fennecs are members of the dog family, so they cannot sweat to cool off as we humans do. Inside the giant ears are special blood vessels that are cooled by the air, which passes through the ears as the fox trots around the desert. The cooled blood travels through the rest of its body, cooling it off.

The second reason for the ears is a more obvious one. Fennecs have excellent hearing, which they depend upon for their survival. Even tiny sounds far away—or far under the desert sand—are picked up by those enormous ears. The fox is able to find food by detecting the slightest, quietest movement of a snake, lizard, rodent, scorpion, bird, or even a tiny insect.

The bottoms of the fennec's feet are covered in fur that protects them from the burning sand. The fur padding also helps the fox to sneak silently across the desert dunes, and to not sink into the sand. Fennecs usually only go out in search of food in the cool morning hours or at night. If they spent too much time out in the unbearable heat of the desert day, they could get too hot and become sick.

DUCK-BILLED PLATYPUS

This creature seems like the result of some crazy science experiment! The duck-billed platypus has webbed feet and a beak, just like a duck. And like a duck, it lays eggs. But it's really a mammal with a furry body that looks more like a beaver's body than anything else! The platypus lives in Australia, where it swims in riverbanks looking for worms, frogs, or shellfish to eat. But it also moves around on land, tucking in the skin of its webbed feet so it can walk easily on the ground.

There's one more weird thing about this guy, and it's something that no duck or beaver shares. Male platypuses have sharp spikes on the heels of their back feet. When an enemy makes a platypus mad, the platypus gives him a jab with that spur, causing poison to shoot out. Yep, this goofy-looking mammal has a secret weapon. Its spike can inject enough venom to kill an animal as big as a dog. People won't die from a prick from a duck-billed platypus, but they can be badly hurt.

TARSIER

Jeepers, creepers, get a load of these peepers! This little weird one is tiny, pop-eyed, and it can fly! Okay, the tarsier can't *really* fly. But it looks like it's flying when it jumps from tree to tree, high up in the forest branches. The tarsier is named for a special third section in its foot that allows it to jump incredible distances. The tarsier is nocturnal—a fancy way to say it sleeps during the day and does its hunting and jumping at night.

A nocturnal cousin of the tarsier is the aye-aye. Aye-ayes are extremely endangered—less than 50 of them may be left on this earth. They're found only on the island of Madagascar, where some people believe that aye-ayes bring bad luck. The weirdest thing about the aye-aye is the third finger on each of its hands. This finger is super skinny and bony and the aye-aye uses it to scoop grubs out from under tree bark.

First the aye-aye taps on the bark and listens for the grubs crawling around within. Then it uses its sharp front teeth to chew a hole in the bark, sticks that bony finger in there, and pulls out some lunch. Yummy! The finger also makes a great utensil for eating coconut out of the shell. And when it's not eating, the aye-aye uses that handy finger to comb its hair!

POLAR BEAR

Beautiful to look at but deadly to tangle with, polar bears are the largest meat-eating animals that walk the Earth. A grown-up male can weigh more than nine men and stand up to ten feet tall. And a polar bear can run much faster than any man can!

Polar bears have two coats of snowy white fur—one long and one short. Both coats are layered with more than four inches of fat to keep the bears warm in the icy regions of the North Pole, where they live. Polar bears have the biggest feet of all eight bear species. Their huge, padded feet are extra-wide—kind of like snowshoes that help them walk in the snow without sinking in. The bottoms of their feet are even covered with a hairy non-skid surface to keep them from slipping on the ice.

Polar bears are expert hunters, with their all-white fur helping them to blend in and hide in the snow. A polar bear might even cover its black nose with its paw when it is sneaking up on its prey! In the summer, if they get too hot in their fur coats, polar bears will dig into the ground to the place where the soil is still frozen. Then they'll lie their huge bodies against the chilly earth to cool off.

PRAIRIE DOG

These friendly little rascals live in huge groups, called towns, all over the grassy plains of western North America. The towns could be as big as 25,000 square miles—that's almost two or three small states put together! A town *that* big could be a home to more than 400 million prairie dogs. The town is divided up into smaller communities (like neighborhoods) called wards, with natural boundaries like streams or hills. Within the wards, prairie dogs live in even smaller family groups called coteries.

A town is made up of a network of tunnels. Each tunnel has two or three entrances. One entrance is usually shaped up into a cone-like crater, giving the prairie dogs a high perch to look out from. If the prairie dog on lookout duty senses any danger, it yaps out a sharp barking call, warning all the other prairie dogs to run as fast as they can back into the safety of their tunnel system.

These good little diggers spend a lot of time building and maintaining their homes, which help them stay warm in the winter and cool in the summer. Somewhere in each tunnel is the family's bedroom, a basketball-sized chamber where the family cuddles up and sleeps. The floor in this "room" is covered with soft fronds, making a cozy bed.

Prairie dogs don't like tall grass because it makes such a good hiding place for their enemies. So they constantly nibble at the grass and plants that surround their home, keeping the area neatly trimmed!

CAMEL

How many humps does a camel have? It depends on the kind of camel!

Bactrian camels have two humps, dromedary camels only have one. Here's a neat trick to help you remember which is which: Picture the capital letter B, lying on its back. Two humps, right? B is for bactrian. Now picture the capital letter D lying on its back. Just one hump for dromedary!

A lot of people think that camels store water in their humps, but the humps are really full of food stored as fat. Camels can go for many days without eating, but when they do, their humps get smaller. They can go even longer without a drink of water—up to six months if the weather is cool.

Camels can live in very harsh conditions where other animals could never survive. If one is caught in a sand or snow storm, it has an extra eyelid that protects its eye. But the eyelid is clear so the camel can see through it, kind of like a windshield on a car. It can also close its nostrils to keep out the sand and snow.

LION

They don't call him the King of the Beasts for nothing! A grown-up male lion can grow longer than a horse and weigh more than 500 pounds. To imagine how big that is, pick up your pet cat and pretend you're holding 50 more just like him. You could hear his thunderous roar even if you were five miles away from this awesome predator.

Lions live in family groups called prides, and the main job of the males is to protect the members of the pride from attack. That's why they have manes and the female lions don't. The mane makes the male lion look bigger and more fierce to help scare enemies away. It also protects his neck from bites or scratches in fights.

So you'd think this king of the beasts would be a big-time hunter, providing his family with plenty of food, right? Wrong! It's the lionesses that do most of the hunting for the pride. They're better at stalking than the guys are because they are lighter and swifter. Plus, the males' manes and larger size make it harder for them to hide and surprise their victims.

Each pride includes adult male lions, lionesses, and cubs. There are usually many more lionesses than lions. The lionesses share the care of one another's cubs. A cub may even nurse from several of the lionesses in the pride. Members of a pride are like a loving, extended family. They'll often say hello by rubbing their bodies against one another and they may snuggle together when they sleep.

One more thing—lions' tongues are covered with hard little spikes for licking the meat off of bones. The spikes are so sharp that a lion can make another animal bleed just by licking it.

GOLDEN LION TAMARIN

Golden lion tamarins are named for their beautiful golden color and the hair around their faces that looks like a lion's mane. When a male and female decide to become mates, they live together for the rest of their lives, only mating with each other.

Family life is very important to tamarins. The family travels together through the trees and shares all aspects of forest life together. Usually a new set of twins—or sometimes triplets—is born every year. The mom can't carry all those babies by herself, so the dad and the older kids help to carry the new babies.

When they stop to sleep or rest, the whole family cuddles up together in a tree. They groom one another with their fingers, and keep each other warm. One might comb through another one's fur, picking out ticks and fly eggs, which it would then eat. Their love for their families is so strong that when a tamarin is captured by humans to be sold as a pet, it will often die just from being separated from its family.

In spite of strong laws against it, tamarins are still trapped and sold for high prices through illegal animal markets. The tamarin is very much endangered.

GIANT PANDA

The panda is one of the best-loved mammals in the world! This big sweetheart lives in China and eats almost nothing but bamboo—a stiff, stalky kind of grass. Grown-up pandas measure about six feet from nose to tail, and can weigh up to 300 pounds. Because of their large size, they have few natural enemies other than man.

A baby panda is born tiny—about the size of a stick of butter. It's so small that the sex of a panda can't be determined until the panda is about four years old! Imagine how weird it would be if you didn't know whether you had a baby brother or a baby sister practically until the kid started kindergarten. The mom holds the itsy-bitsy baby in the palm of her hand for at least four weeks, hardly ever putting it down. When the baby is hungry, the mom panda just holds it up to her breast to nurse.

Pandas really do look like big, cuddly teddy bears, and you've probably heard them called panda bears. But they're actually not bears at all. In the animal kingdom, they are in a group all their own.

ORANGUTAN

Can you guess how the orangutan got its name? If you guessed it was named for its color, you'd be wrong. Orangutans ARE orange, but their name comes from a native word meaning "people of the forest." And they really do seem a lot like people!

Orangutans in the wild communicate with one another with gestures and sounds. When they are playing or are being tickled, they make noises that sound like laughter. Some observers of orangs claim they are the most intelligent of all land animals. Since they are good at imitation, they are often trained for circuses or for parts in movies.

Orangutans have 32 teeth, just like you! Mom orangutans nurse their babies just like human moms, and they comb their babies' hair with their fingers, pulling out dirt and bugs, and working out tangles. They even trim their babies nails with their teeth!

But unlike us, orangutans spend most of their lives up in the trees. Their hands are very big and strong, with long fingers that can wrap completely around a branch or vine, locking in place so that the orang can easily support its entire body weight with one hand. Orangs can swing from tree to tree and move faster through the treetops than a person can run on the ground! Mostly vegetarian, they love to eat ripe fruit. They are gentle and usually will not attack people unless they are threatened.

HUMAN BEING

If any other animal were writing this book, I bet WE would top the list of weird ones. Here are some facts about humans—possibly the weirdest mammals of all—from the *Guinness Book of World Records:*

· A human guy grew a mustache over eight feet long.
· Another human collected over 6,000 four-leaf clovers.
· Another one turned over 8,000 somersaults in a row, covering a distance of over 12 miles.
· One made a 12,105-foot gum wrapper chain.
· And one weird human has eaten ten bicycles, a supermarket cart, seven TV sets, six chandeliers, a computer, a coffin and a Cessna aircraft. The doctors don't know why he can do it. Eating metal and glass would make the rest of us VERY SICK, so don't try this weirdness yourself!

Well, you're the judge!
Who's the weirdest of them all?

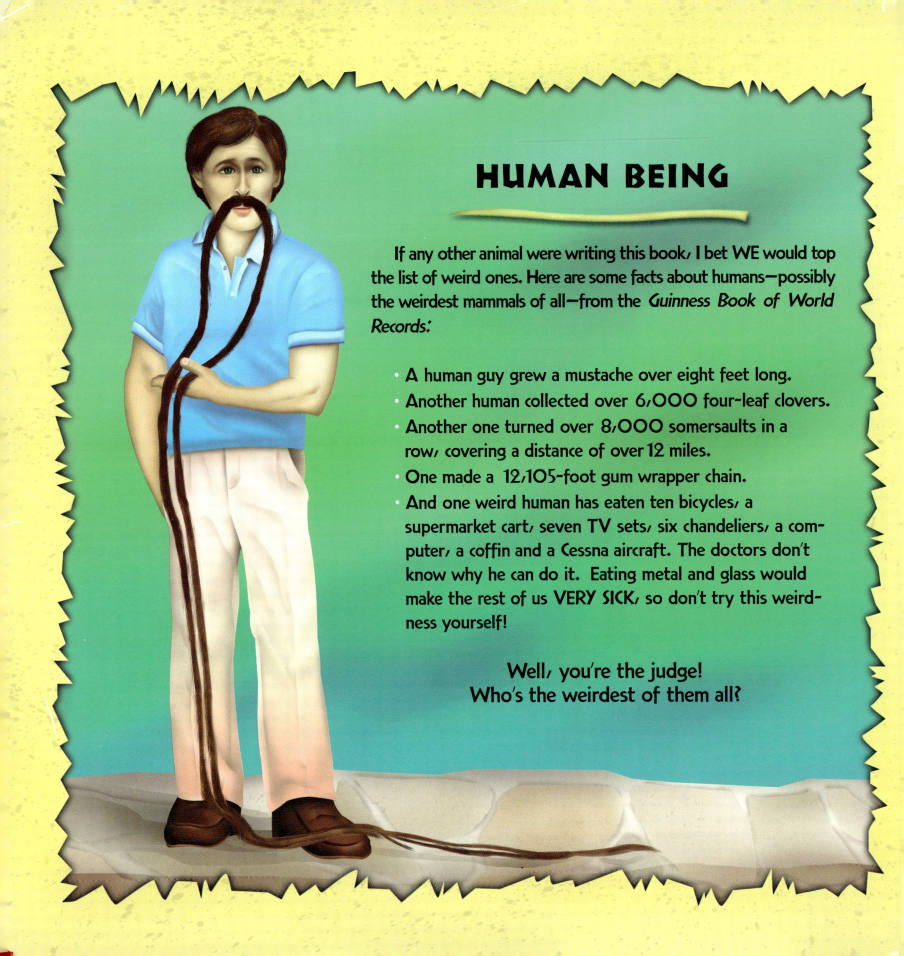